Elixir For Pain & Love

Expressions of the soul

Aditi Tiwari

BookLeaf Publishing

India | USA | UK

Made with ❤ on the BookLeaf Publishing Platform
www.bookleafpub.in
www.bookleafpub.com

Dedication

Dedicated to the boy & girl who lives within

To the souls who have loved so deeply they became fire,
To the seekers who have prayed so fiercely they
shattered,
To those who have tasted either love or divinity—only to
learn there is no return.

This collection is for you.
For the ones who understand that love and spirit are
twin flames, both demanding surrender, both baptizing
in suffering, both leading—through agony, through
ecstasy—to an eternity from which there is no escape.
May these words be your crucible and your elixir, your
undoing and your awakening. May they remind you that
once touched by the divine or by love, you are no longer
who you were. You are something more. Something
infinite.
May these verses be an elixir for your journey—a
whisper in the dark, a light on the path, a hand upon
your heart.
With devotion,
Aditi Tiwari

Preface

Poetry is born where the heart aches and heals, where love lingers beyond time, and where the hand of the divine brushes against the soul.

These verses have come to me not as mere words, but as whispers from something greater—wind through the trees, the hush of snowfall, the pull of the tide. They have come from moments of quiet wonder, from love that felt older than this life, from grief that carved its name into my bones, and from the stillness where the universe sings.

We do not walk alone. The stars have known us before we knew ourselves, and the earth hums with the stories we are only beginning to understand. Love is the thread that weaves us through lifetimes, guiding us back to one another, over and over again, until at last, we dissolve into the divine.

I have looked to nature for answers, and it has shown me that all we seek is already within us.

The river does not question where it flows; the leaves do not fear the fall. There is a pattern to it all, a rhythm that only the heart can hear if it dares to listen. These poems are my listening. If they find you in a moment of stillness, if they echo something already stirring inside you, then perhaps we are both hearing the same song. And perhaps, in the grand design of things, we were always meant to.

Read them with an open heart. Let them find you. Let them remind you of what you already know: that love is the language of the universe, and it is calling your name.

May these poems find you when you need them. May they remind you that you are never truly lost. That love, in all its forms, is proof that something greater moves through us. That we are here to find each other. To feel each other. To live. And, in the end, to return to the divine.

— Aditi Tiwari

Acknowledgements

With a heart overflowing with gratitude, I bow to the forces—seen and unseen—that have shaped this journey, allowing me to weave my soul into words. *Elixir of Pain and Love* is not merely a collection of poems; it is a piece of my heart, a whisper of my soul, and a reflection of all that I have lived, loved, and endured.

I am eternally grateful to my parents Shri. Pradeep Kumar Shukla and Smt. Lata Shukla, who gifted me this life, nurturing me with love and values that continue to guide my path. To my husband, Goldy—my rock, my safe haven—your unwavering faith in me, your patience, love, and boundless support allow me to be my truest self. In every word I write, I feel the confidence you instill in me, and for that, I am forever indebted.

To our children, Abhishek and Prasanna, my greatest blessings—you are my heartbeats, my inspiration, and my constant source of love. Your belief in me gives my words the strength to soar. My mother-in-law, Mrs. Archana Tiwari, has been my guiding light, showering me with encouragement and love, giving me the courage to step into the world of poetry and find my voice. And to my brother, Pramil—your excitement for all my endeavours, no matter how big or small, fills me with warmth and motivation.

I bow in reverence to my guru, Shri Morari Bapu, whose teachings of truth, love, and compassion have become the essence of my being, shaping not just my poetry but my very existence.

A special place in my heart is reserved for Dr. Sheetal Nair "Siddh," my strength, my guiding star, my best friend for life. You not only showed me the path but walked beside me, lighting the way with your wisdom and belief in me. Without you, this book would have remained just a dream.

To the poetic community and every soul who chooses to read these words—this is my first attempt to bare my soul through poetry, and your encouragement means the world to me. Every word of support, every moment of resonance, will be the wind beneath my wings, urging me to write more, to share more, to express more.

From the depths of my heart, I am grateful for every opportunity, every hand that held mine, and every voice that whispered, *keep going*. This book exists because of you all.

With love and gratitude,

Aditi Tiwari

1. Beyond the Boundaries

When two hearts meet, unshackled, free,
No walls remain 'twixt you and me.
No chains can bind, no border stand,
For love's a tide, not ruled by hand.

Can you command the wind to stay,
Or halt the sun upon its way?
Can you seize air, or hold the seas?
So is love's will—not bent to please.

The lines we draw, the fences high,
Are shadows cast by fear's weak eye.
For when love's truth breaks through the night,
The self dissolves in boundless light.

No "mine" or "yours," no place apart,
No space remains in such a heart.
It flows like rivers—deep, profound,
It knows no edge, no stake of ground.

In love, there is no loss, no gain,
No self to clutch, no need to reign.
For love's true strength, its richest art,
Is found when souls dissolve in heart.

So let us soar, as air does move,
No need to grasp, no need to prove.
For love, unbound, will always be
A force as vast as sky or sea.

2. A Whisper of Tomorrow

If life should pass, a fleeting breeze,
And leave me standing 'neath the trees,
Where others forged and carved their way,
I lingered, watching their display.

The love I sought, a distant star,
Shone bright, yet always stayed afar.
Its light was warm, its pull was strong,
Yet silence kept me bound too long.

Ambition knocked upon my door,
I raised no hand, I strove no more.
A bystander, I watched the tide,
While others fought, I stepped aside.

The future looms, a shrouded veil,
Its course unknown, its winds may fail.
But somewhere in that murky stream,
Perhaps there lies another dream.

Another chance, another role,
To mend the wounds, uplift the soul.
To find the purpose, deep and true,
Before my days are faded through.

For here on earth, though trials tear,
The meaning waits, perhaps somewhere.
And may it come, that truth so near,
Before the end draws stark and clear.

So, onward still, though time does wane,
Through love, through loss, through joy and pain.
The tale's not told, the path's not set,
And hope, my friend, remains yet met.

3. The Silent Ache

Loneliness is not the hollow of space,
Nor the stillness that shadows an empty place.
It is the cry of a heart that longs to share,
Yet turns to find no listening there.

It is the joy of a thought, bright and new,
That fades unspoken, for there are too few
Who understand the spark, the fire, the flame—
And silence answers when you call a name.

It's the taste of something rare, exquisite, fine,
That begs for two to savor the wine.
The ache when you turn with a smile so wide,
But the echo is nothing, for none are beside.

It's the thrill of an idea, fragile, bright,
That withers untold in the absence of light.
For a mind needs another, a kindred, a friend,
To hold what the soul alone cannot bend.

Loneliness is not in the absence of sound,
But the absence of care, where love once was found.
It's the weight of words that will never be heard,
The sting of emotion left unexplored.

For a man is not stone, though strength he may feign,
He is rivers and winds, and he bleeds in the rain.
He is laughter and longing, a soft, fragile thread,
A being who aches when connections are dead.

So seek not a crowd, nor a throne, nor a fame,
But the one who will call you again by your name.
For all we desire, through sorrow and strife,
Is a soul who will share the burden of life.

And when you have found them, hold them with care,
For the ache of their absence is too much to bear.

4. Ode to My Pillow, My Lover

You, soft keeper of my secrets,
Catch my joy, my confusion, my pain.
You cradle the ache of love unspoken,
The electric hum of desire,
And the sweet whispers of dreams
Born and broken.

A silent lover, you know it all—
The restless toss of longing nights,
The fevered storm of sleepless fights,
The warmth of tender, tearful cuddles,
Where heartache pools into quiet puddles.
I bury my face in your embrace,
Where your quiet holds the storm at bay.
You are my solace, my steadfast balm,
My midnight witness, my lover's calm.

You absorb my battles, my tender confessions,
The softest anchor to my obsessions.

I fight you, clutch you, beg you to stay,
And still you are here,
At the close of the day.
With whispered goodnights, I fall into you,
My sweetest comfort, my endless muse.

5. The flame of us

Beneath the moon's soft glow, where silence lies,
You are the breath that stirs the night's soft sighs.
In every glance, a spark, a flame ignites,
Your touch, a symphony that thrills the nights.

My soul, a canvas, painted by your grace,
Each kiss a brushstroke, leaving no trace.
Your eyes, twin stars that pull me from the dark,
Guiding me to depths where love leaves its mark.

With every whisper, every heated glance,
You set my heart ablaze in passionate dance.
Your lips, a promise, each one laced in fire,
Fulfilling every longing, every desire.

In your embrace, I find my soul's release,
You are the quiet to my storm's fierce peace.
Together, we complete a world so vast—
In you, my heart is found, and love will last.

6. The Elixir of Pain and Love

Pain, our shadow, steadfast and true,
It whispers, reminds, what matters to you.
A companion unyielding, through night and day,
It teaches, it shapes, in its own cruel way.

Though nothing lasts, we cling to the fire,
The warmth of love, our deepest desire.
Yet love's embrace sharpens the ache,
A bittersweet longing we cannot forsake.

Lose yourself in its tender snare,
But pain will find you, it's always there.
Still, within the depths of sorrow's embrace,
Hope quietly lingers, offering grace.

When the divine smiles upon your plea,
A lover may come, setting you free.
One who sees you, your essence, your soul,
Who mends the fragments, making you whole.

In their love, the pain will subside,
The sad smile replaced, joy amplified.
And in that elixir, a life anew,
You'll need nothing else, just love's purest truth.

7. Shattered Bonds

Shattered bonds linger,
love's fibres woven through time,
yet drift, unbroken.

We could have fled, hand in hand,
To somewhere quiet, a promised land.
No snapping words, no bitter shove,
No shooing away what once was love.

I mattered once; I mattered then,
Before the breaking, before the end.
Yet now I stand, a hollowed shell,
Carrying your ghost in every cell.

Was it my fault, this shattered frame?
Did I bear too much of love's cruel flame?
To let you go, to break, to sever,
Feels like unlearning how to breathe forever.

You lived in me, in thought, in prayer,

In every choice, in every care.
To die would seem the softer plea
Than to unlive this life without thee.

Yet here I stand, a shadowed thing,
A bird with broken, unfeathered wings.
Dreaming of what we might have been—
Of love unlost, of a life unseen.

8. The Tides of Love

"Out of sight is out of mind,"
A saying oft by reason blind.
For love, it lingers, soft yet strong,
A tune that hums a ceaseless song.

It veils the eyes, yet clears the soul,
Binding hearts beyond control.
In every thought, it softly weaves,
A trace of joy, a touch of grief.

The beloved's name, a whispered breeze,
That stirs the mind with gentle tease.
Their absence, though, becomes the sea,
Where waves crash hard incessantly.

As tides retreat, then rush once more,
They batter on the heart's own shore.
With every surge, the ache grows deep,
A love awake, it cannot sleep.

For time and space, mere fleeting lies,
When love is seen through blindfolded eyes.
Though worlds apart, the heart will find,
That love defies both space and time.

9. Eclipsed Love

Our love burns like fire, a smoldering glow,
Deep with desire where no eyes may know.
Buried in shadows, yet fervent and bright,
A secret that shimmers in veils of the night.

Clandestine whispers in moonlight confined,
A love that is hidden, yet endlessly kind.
Concealed in the hush of the stars' gentle sighs,
A passion unbroken where secrecy lies.

Covered in silence, yet loud in the heart,
An uncharted longing that won't fall apart.
Underground rivers carve deep through the stone,
Though hidden from sight, we are never alone.

Unknown to the world, yet profound and true,
Like the sun veiled in darkness, yet burning for you.
Though eclipsed by the night, love's promise won't sever,
For even in shadow, we shine on—forever.

10. The Life Before Me

There was a life before me, he said.
Yes, I thought—there was a life.

A life of laughter, rolling like tides,
crashing against the quiet ache of solitude.
A life of faces—so many faces—
each one familiar, yet none my own.

I lived in rooms too grand to hold me,
in halls echoing with the sound of my name,
a name spoken with admiration, with judgment,
with curiosity that never truly asked.
I was seen by all, known by none,
a ghost in the house I called home.

There were parties—oh, the endless dance—
champagne fizzing, laughter spinning,
celebrations painted in gold and silk.
I was the rhythm, the pulse of the night,
the one who made the world shimmer,

yet inside, nothing stirred.

I lived a life people would die for,
but it was no different for me.

I missed the hush of my own breath,
the quiet truth of a smile meant only for me.
I missed love—not the kind that watched
from across a crowded room,
but the kind that whispered in the dark,
that held my hand when no one else could see.

I missed my mind, sharp and unbroken,
my ambition, wild and untamed.
I missed the honor of honesty,
the fire of true laughter,
the poetry of being free.

To be seen—not adorned, but understood.
To be heard—not praised, but believed.
To be loved—not admired, but known.

Yes, I thought to myself—
before all this, I had a life.
And somewhere beneath it all,

I still do.

11. Shattered Trust

You love, you trust-"oh, how you trust-"
Clinging to every crack with a desperate *why,*
Battered by silence, bruised by doubt,
Yet refusing to heed the whisper inside.

You drown in denial, fight against fate,
Holding tight when the world says let go,
Bleeding from wounds you pretend aren't there,
Hoping against hope they don't grow.

But then - the blow. Not a crack, not a tear,
But a ruinous shatter, a merciless fall.
The ground is gone, your name is dust,
And worst of all - you don't know you at all.

The mirror mocks, the echoes sneer,
Were you blind? Were you a fool?
Doubt coils tight like a serpent's grip,
Every memory now cruel.

And so, you rise-barely, broken,
Gathering pieces of who you were.
You swear to never forgive, never forget,
Yet the ache remains- a ghost, a blur.

For trust once shattered is trust forever,
And though time may dull the sting,
The lesson stays, the scar remains,
And love..will never feel the same.

12. When You Love a Person

When you love a person,
you don't just hold them—you become them.
They slip beneath your skin,
thread themselves through your veins,
press their breath into your lungs
until every exhale tastes like their name.
They live in your thoughts,
in the tilt of your laughter,
in the quiet pull of your soul toward theirs.
You seek them in every shadow,
in every echo of a voice,
in the spaces where their absence
turns the world a shade dimmer.

Their eyes meet yours,
and the earth steadies,
a tether, a home, a gravity
that no force can undo.
Only their presence reassures,
only their touch revives.

Their fragrance lingers—intoxicating,
their pull—inescapable.
Magnetic, consuming, burning.
A storm that swallows you whole,
yet somehow makes you feel
like you were never more complete.

Because when you love a person,
they do not stay outside of you—
they devour you, inhabit you,
and nothing—nothing—feels whole without them.
When you love a person,
they don't just stay in your life—
they become it.

13. Moonlight's Spell

The night spills silver on the earth,
A hush of light, a quiet birth.
The river shivers in its glow,
Soft ripples sighing, deep and slow.

A breath of cold, a ghostly hand,
It grips the trees, it sweeps the land.
A fleeting chill upon my skin,
The moon's own whisper, drawing in.

The full moon looms—an eye, a face,
An ageless watcher, lost in space.
It sees us love, it sees us leave,
It hears the songs, it mourns, it grieves.

A poet's muse, a lover's guide,
A child's first wonder, wild and wide.
It bends the waves, it shapes the night,
It moves the heart, it fuels the fight.

And though it shines with borrowed grace,
Reflected light, a phantom's trace,
It holds a power, fierce and bright—
To shake the soul, to stir, to write.

But time runs thin; the night won't stay,
The dawn will steal the moon away.
Yet for a moment, here we stand,
Bathed in its glow—hand in hand.

14. Garden of Souls

There is a place beyond the veil,
where silence sings and love prevails.
No hunger calls, no thirst remains,
just endless being, free of chains.

No shape, no form, yet all is known,
each soul a light, yet not alone.
No walls divide, no need to hide,
pure essence flows, no fear inside.

In this garden, time stands still,
no want, no ache, no force of will.
Only bliss—a boundless sea,
dancing in divinity.

Yet sometimes souls will yearn to feel,
to touch, to hold, to dream what's real.
They drift as whispers to the earth,
to taste again, to give rebirth.

To sing, to laugh, to weep, to dance,
to live within love's sweet expanse.
And when you find that sacred one,
a soul remembered, not just won—

Know this truth, so soft, so bright,
they stood with you in golden light.
A partner lost, now found anew,
from the garden, back to you.

15. Echoes of Absence

Your absence is a scream trapped in my chest,
a voice that breaks against my ribs,
echoing, echoing,
where silence gnaws the edges of my breath.

My heart beats to every sound,
every shadow, every shift of air,
as if it might be you,
as if you might return,
as if the universe might fold itself in mercy
and place you back into my hands.

But the truth strikes sharp—
you are not here.
And the knowing carves deep,
splitting me open from soul to skin,
spilling grief in heavy sobs
that shake the walls of my bones.

The tears come violent, unstoppable,

as if they could drown the ache,
as if the flood could carry me to you—
but all it does is leave me gasping,
breathless, broken,
lost in the wreckage of what was.

I crave you like air,
but you are the storm that stole it.
I reach for you in darkness,
but you are the night that swallowed me whole.
I whisper your name,
lips trembling, voice unraveling—
but only silence answers,
cruel and endless,
mocking the space where you used to be.

16. Mirror of My Soul, Divine and True

O mirror of soul, the divine you are,
A presence so near, yet distant as stars.
Ever beside me, unseen yet known,
A light in my darkness, a guide when I'm thrown.

You whisper in silence, you thunder in thought,
A wellspring of wisdom so endlessly sought.
I call you by names—one or many,
Yet you answer, patient as any.

You see me falter, you see me rise,
With love unshaken, with watchful eyes.
You do not bind, nor pull my strings,
You simply offer—endless wings.

My will is mine, yet shaped by you,
With choices vast, both old and new.
You teach me truth, yet let me stray,
For lessons shine in night and day.

You are my compass, my shadow bright,
My silent muse, my inner light.
You do not force, you gently show,
The path that waits, the way to grow.

In you, I see a boundless sea,
A mirrored glimpse of divinity.
As I reflect, so do you,
A radiance pure, a love so true.
O mirror fair, my soul's embrace,
In you, I find my truest place.

17. Bittersweet Joy

Oh, how I long for you—
a hunger unquenched, a thirst ever new.
How I ache to drown in your eyes,
to fold into your arms,
to taste the honey of your lips
until time itself forgets to move.

How I burn to feel your touch,
to be filled, to be set ablaze,
to surrender beneath the weight of you—
but alas, you know nothing of this fire.
You walk, unknowing, untouched,
while I am scorched by every glance,
consumed by every whisper of your presence.

What cruel delight, what aching joy,
to see you, to feel you,
to want you with every breath—
yet never to claim you as mine.
For you are the moon, distant and divine,

and I am but the tide,
forever pulled, forever denied.

Tell me, love—
if you knew the depths of my torment,
if you felt the storm that rages within me,
would you turn away?
Or would you drown with me
in this beautiful, bitter abyss?

18. Tidal Grief

Tears don't stop—they surge like vengeful waves,
Relentless, wild, in sorrow's endless crave.
They crash upon the fragile shore of my heart,
Tearing its edges, ripping it apart.

The salty sting of memories, half-submerged,
Rises like ghosts when the tide is urged.
Whispers of laughter, now brittle, now thin,
Echo from the depths of what once had been.

The shore, once soft with warmth and grace,
Now bears the scars of time's cold embrace.
Each wave a mourner draped in gray,
Carrying yesterday's light away.

The sun dares not break through this grief-stained sky;
It watches, helpless, as I drown, as I cry.
The winds, complicit, howl through the night,
Mocking my hope, extinguishing light.

And yet—oh, cruel trick of fate's design—
The waves retreat, and hope aligns.
Only to return with savage might,
To haunt, to shatter, to steal the night.

No peace in this eternal ebb and flow,
Where love once lived, and sorrow grows.
The sea of loss knows no end, no cease—
Only the aching dream of peace.

19. The Paradox of Love

A heart that burns, yet fate's cruel chain,
Keeps passion bound in silent pain.
Days drift by, a hollowed haze,
Nights weep soft in shadowed maze.
Why crave a touch you'll never own?
Why love a ghost, forever known?

They ask, with voices sharp and clear,
"Why chase what can't draw near?"
But hearts know truths the mind disdains—
Love blooms best in hopeless rains.
To want, to ache, to break anew,
For someone life won't yield to you.

The soul, relentless, bends, won't break,
Drawn to depths where dreams forsake.
The more it hopes, the more it dies,
Beneath the weight of endless skies.
To live, to long, to love in vain—
A beautiful, exquisite pain.

What madness lingers, what curse, what art?
To tie such sorrow to a heart?
Yet still, you love—despite, because—
No reason, logic, rule, or cause.
For love defies what fate commands—
It writes in tears with trembling hands.

And so you break, each day, each night—
Haunted by that distant light.
A love that cannot, will not be—
Yet owns your soul completely, endlessly.

20. Soul in Peace (SIP)

Born, lived, loved—then died, they say,
A fleeting breath, a borrowed stay.
The endless cycle, turning still,
Time bends to life's unyielding will.
Chaos dances in shadows deep,
While restless hearts forget to weep.

We chase the glimmer, the fleeting flame—
A name, a face, a whispered fame.
Moments grasped, yet slipping fast,
Like echoes of a distant past.
The world screams: *More!*—we heed its call,
Blind to the rise, deaf to the fall.

Is it wealth? Is it pride? A crown of gold?
The stories of glory that we are told?
Or legacy, etched on brittle stone—
To prove we mattered once, alone?
We run, we grasp, we bleed, we break,
For illusions we refuse to forsake.

But pause—breathe—look within.
Where the quiet soul has always been.
No fame, no face, no fleeting prize—
Just endless skies in inward eyes.
The answer, soft as twilight's grace,
Is found in stillness we dare not face.

Sit in peace—just *be*, not strive.
Feel the pulse of all alive.
The stars, the sea, the earth, the air—
Divine whispers everywhere.
Not in the chase, nor in the climb,
But in surrender, beyond time.

So sip this peace, this sacred art—
Let silence mend your weary heart.
Born, lived, loved—and yes, we die,
Yet the soul, serene, learns to fly.
No chains, no race, no fleeting chase—
Just endless grace in timeless space.

21. My Love

My love,
What words dare touch the vastness of what I feel?
One glance from you—like lightning cleaving the night—
And I was lost, willingly, eternally, without a map or
mercy.
From that moment, my heart was no longer mine;
It became yours—a silent offering at the altar of your
existence.

Your touch, oh, your touch—
A spark that surged through my veins, igniting a fire no
ocean could quell.
One caress, and time collapsed; worlds faded into
shadows.
There is no taste, no sound, no breath without the
memory of you.
You are the tempest that stirs my soul, the calm that
soothes it afterward.

Is it madness to love like this? To ache, to yearn with

such ferocity?
To feel the echo of you even in your absence,
As though the universe itself etched your name into my
very marrow?
If so, let me stay mad, for sanity holds no allure in a
world without you.

This love—ours—is not bound by flesh, nor confined by
time.
It is a force, ancient and infinite, written in the stars
before we ever met.
We are not mere mortals caught in fleeting passion;
We are souls entwined, dancing through lifetimes,
beyond the reach of reason.

Unexplainable, undeniable, and utterly enigmatic—
This love defies logic, mocks explanation.
It simply is.
And in its depth, its fury, its quiet, eternal grace,
I find the meaning of my existence.
You. Always, only you.